Tee Two and His Horse Sparkle

by

Alvin D Walker Jr

Illustrations by **Ayan Mansoori**

ISBN: 978-1-7378051-6-8 (Digital online)

ISBN: 978-1-7378051-7-5 (Paperback)

ISBN: 978-1-7378051-8-2 (Hardcover)

Library of Congress Control Number: In Public Data

Walker, Alvin

Any references to historical events, real people, or real places are used fictitiously. Names, characters, and places are products of the author's imagination.

Front cover image by Ayan Mansoori

Images by Ayan Mansoori

Printed in the United States of America.

First printing edition 2021.

Publisher by Alvin Walker

Contact Info: Bigidea62@gmail.com

My Book

My Name:

_____

My Age:

_____

My Address:

_____

Dedication:

This book was written from the heart for my little grandson. He is only seven but is in such a hurry to grow up.

Love you Tee Two,

Papaw

About Author

Hello, my name is Alvin Walker. I am a sixty-three-year-old retiree. Who has just started living life to the fullish? My kids and grandkids are the best things that ever happened to me. My family and I do a lot of traveling. We really enjoy spending time with my grandchildren. `

Contents_Toc82539509

Introduction

The bonding between a young seven years old boy named Tee Two and his horse named Sparkle. Sparkle is medium size brownness horse with a black main. This book is about Tee Two taking care of his horse daily. In the process, he learns reasonability and to care for others. Not to just think only about himself.

Chapter 1

Tee Two waking up in the morning early to take care of Sparkle

It's early Saturday morning when a little boy woke up thinking of a horse named Sparkle. He rushes to the bathroom to wash his face, brush his teeth, comb his hair and take a shower, all in about ten minutes. His mother calls out to him Tee Two, your breakfast is ready. Tee Two replies to his mother I don't have time, mom. I have to go feed Sparkle.

Chapter 2

Tee Two Feeding Sparkle

The moment Sparkle saw Tee Two. Sparkle screams out with this incredible horse whinny. I think Sparkle was so glad to see Tee Two, maybe because she knows he is going to feed her, perhaps because she was just glad to see him. Tee Two greeted Sparkle by rubbing her on the center of her head and petting her on her neck in a loving and kind way. Tee Two says to Sparkle, "I will take care of you, girl. "Then Tee Two goes to the storage shed and puts out a bag of feed then takes it to Sparkle's feed trough. He also takes Sparkle a bay of hay.

Chapter 3

Tee Two Cleaning Sparkle Pen

Tee Two's least favorite job about taking care of Sparkle is cleaning up behind her. It is a very dirty job, but someone got to do it. Tee Two found out early that the more you feed Sparkle, the more he has to clean out her pen. Sparkle follows Tee Two around as if she is supervising him.

Chapter 4

Tee Two Riding Sparkle

Tee Two's most favorite thing to do is to ride Sparkle. Sparkle is such a gentle horse. She makes sure that she doesn't hurt Tee Two. If Tee Two happens to fall off, she will stop and stay with Tee Two. Tee Two rides Sparkle for most of the day.

Chapter 5

Tee Two Rubbing Sparkle Down After Riding

Tee Two always rubs Sparkle down with a brush after riding her. Sparkle really enjoys the rub-down, and with every brush, Sparkle loves Tee Two more. Tee Two takes very good care of Sparkle.

Chapter 6

Tee Two Watering and Feeds Sparkle for Bed

Tee Two always gives Sparkle clean water and a good feeding at the end of the day.

Tee Two always receives that long stare and a loud horse whinny from Sparkle when he turns and walks away out of sight.

Chapter 7

Sparkle has a visit from the Veterinarian Twice a Year

Sparkle has a visit from the Veterinarian twice a year, and Tee Two is there to help. The Veterinarian looks at the horse's teeth and worms Sparkle. Tee Two holds Sparkle's mouth open while the Veterinarian shoots the pill into Sparkle's mouth using a pill gun.

Chapter .8

Tee Two has Sparkle's Hooves files and Trim.

Tee Two uses a professional person as a farrier to do Sparkle's hooves. He trims and smooths out the edges of hooves and then places them on the horse's shoes. Tee Two looks on to learn how one day to do it on his own.

Chapter 9

Tee Two always makes sure Sparkle's new shoes are comfortable

Tee Two walks Sparkle around on the road and the field to see if the new horseshoe is a good fix. He makes sure Sparkle doesn't have a limp.

Chapter 10

Tee Two keeps Sparkle's Sable with Clean Bedding

Tee Two uses Hay for Sparkle's bedding, so Sparkle would have a clean, dry place to lay down for the night.

Conclusion

The bond between a young boy and his horse can be a strong one and one that Tee Two will remember for the rest of his life when he learns to work hard to take care of a friend.

The End

www.ingramcontent.com/pod-product-compliance
Lightning Source LLC
Chambersburg PA
CBHW042106040426

42448CB00002B/158